Transcendental Meditation: Powerful Transcendental Meditation Guide -Improve Work Efficiency and Creativity While Reducing Chronic Stress and Anxiety

by S.J. Morgan

Disclaimer

TABLE OF CONTENTS

Free Bonus Gift

As a special thank you for downloading and purchasing this book I would like to offer you an exclusive free eBook about "Law of Attraction 101" which I believe can personally believe can help anybody achieve their dreams.

If you want to take your life to another level, and become the ultimate manifester and truly learn the stepping blocks of mastering the law of attraction then this guide book will help tremendously.

In this free eBook you will learn the 25 little steps that can bring you massive results.

>>> DOWNLOAD THIS FREE EBOOK BY CLICKING HERE<<<

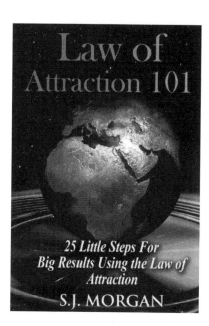

Introduction

Over a couple of last decades the fan following of Transcendental Meditation is growing at rapidly. A large number of famous personalities and celebrities are practitioners of Transcendental Meditation. The practitioners of Transcendental Meditation belong to different parts of the world. The Transcendental Meditation community is very diverse in terms of faith, educational qualification, profession, geographical location and cultures background. It is most popular in Western cultures and Hindu cultures and Buddhist cultures. Even the Transcendental Meditation is equally famous among the people who do not believe in GOD or any religion. Buddhism is prevalent in Asian countries.

All though a significant number of Buddhist people also live in Americas, Europe, Africa and Australia. The countries with more than 5 million populations are India, China, Japan, North Korea, South Korea, Vietnam, Malaysia, Myanmar, Cambodia and Thailand. Hinduism is prevalent in Asian countries. All though a significant number of Hindu people also live in Americas, Europe, Africa and Australia. The countries with more than 500,000 populations are India, Nepal, Mauritius, Indonesia, Pakistan, Sri Lanka, United States, Malaysia, Myanmar, United Kingdom and South Africa. After this brief introduction of the topic, we will now move to next chapter to see the historical background of the Transcendental Medication.

Then it describes what Transcendental Meditation is not. Later it has explained how Transcendental Meditation is different and what happens during Transcendental Meditation. It also explains whether how we know Transcendental Meditation is working. Later we will discuss what research and science says about Transcendental Meditation followed by effects Transcendental Meditation on the brain. Techniques for Transcendental Meditation make this book unique and valuable. In the last part, this book discusses why Transcendental Meditation works for everyone. Famous

Practitioners Transcendental Meditation and Famous Quotes on Transcendental Meditation are also mentioned to motivate our readers. Over a couple of last decades the fan following of Transcendental Meditation is growing at rapidly.

A large number of famous personalities and celebrities are practitioners of Transcendental Meditation. The practitioners of Transcendental Meditation belong to different parts of the world. The Transcendental Meditation community is very diverse in terms of faith, educational qualification, profession, geographical location and cultures background. It is most popular in Western cultures and Hindu cultures and Buddhist cultures. Even the Transcendental Meditation is equally famous among the people who do not believe in GOD or any religion.

Chapter 1: History of Transcendental Meditation

Where it came from

Although the history of meditation dates back to thousands of years ago when people we used to sit still and with eyes closed to get powers. Meditation is an important ritual in many religions. . Majority of us know that the traditional act of meditation is present in Hinduism and Buddhism. Both Hinduism and Buddhism are of the view that very amazing results can be obtained by practicing meditation sincerely. It is not a mere claim.

The process of meditation is indeed amazing experience that enriches the practitioner with spiritual energy. Meditation also caters the need of human beings to obtain internal peace and peace of mind through a regular session of meditation on daily basis. Although meditation refers to a simple method of sitting with eyes closed for several minutes but nevertheless, there are different methods to practice mediation. In 1955, an Indian, Mr. Maharishi

Mahesh Yogi came up with an new version of the meditation through Transcendental Meditation Movement. He learned this meditation form his master Brahmananda Saraswati. It was denoted as "Transcendental Deep Meditation" but later this new version of Meditation known to be "Transcendental Meditation".

Mr. Maharishi Mahesh Yogi later started to teach Transcendental Meditation in India. Soon this idea gained popularity and Mr. Maharishi Mahesh Yogi started to deliver lecture on Transcendental Meditation in other countries and this amazing method of getting self peace gained popularity dramatically. Mr. Maharishi Mahesh Yogi taught this meditation to thousands of people and established a training program to produce the people who can transfer this knowledge to others. Soon his idea got popularity in people from all walk of life and from all cultures. Soon many famous personalities started to practice Transcendental Meditation and started to endorsement Transcendental Meditation in public. Due to this reason its popularity and followers increased many folds. The successor to Mr. Maharishi Mahesh Yogi and Global Country of World Peace is Tony Nader.

International Meditation Society and Spiritual Regeneration Movement were the first organizations to promote Transcendental Meditation. in present time, this movement has started to enter into the curriculum of the schools, colleges and universities of some countries. There are a large number of organizations and societies run by individuals to promote Transcendental Meditation. In this chapter, we have discussed History of Transcendental Meditation. In the next chapter we will discuss what Transcendental Meditation is.

Chapter 2: What is Transcendental Meditation?

By Transcendental Meditation we mean a specific form of mantra based meditation which is known as Transcendental Meditation Technique. Transcendental Meditation also refers to organizations that work under the Transcendental Meditation Movement umbrella and to Transcendental Meditation technique Movement itself. We have discussed in first chapter that this technique was introduced by Mr. Maharishi Mahesh Yogi in 1955.

Mr. Maharishi Mahesh Yogi was a very energetic person with a dynamic personality. He worked day and night to promote this new type of meditation to the world. He achieved this goal and when he died in 2008, this meditation was being practiced by millions of people around the world. Mr. Maharishi enriched thousands of people with this meditation from a series of tours to other countries from 1958 to 1965. He was used to spread his views on meditation in a spiritual and religious way. The popularity of Transcendental Meditation multiplied in the decades from 1960s to 1970s.

Then Mr. Maharishi started to promote Transcendental Meditation in more technical way and due to this many famous personalities started to follow Transcendental Meditation. Then he began training Transcendental Meditation to people who were interested to teach it to other people. To teach these people he established specialized organizations to teach Transcendental Meditation to future teachers. By the time of his death (in 2008), he had taught to millions of people and his worldwide Transcendental Meditation organization had started to offer educational programs, health products and related services.

It is too much easy to practice Transcendental Meditation. The Transcendental Meditation method involves use of sound mantra and is practiced for 15 – 20 minutes consecutively. There are a large number of Transcendental Meditation teachers around the world who are dedicatedly teaching Transcendental Meditation techniques. It is well established fact that Transcendental Meditation is a method for relaxation, stress reduction and self-development. With increasing popularity of Transcendental Meditation, scholars and sociologist are more inclined to conduct research on Transcendental Meditation. some people try to prove it religiously motivated, whereas, others associate is non-religious views.

Due to the struggle of Mr. Maharishi and his disciples, Transcendental Meditation has become one of the widely practiced, most widely researched meditation techniques. Some scholars does not accept that Transcendental Meditation has any significant affects on human health as the data to support it is not reliable. Some scientists have proved with experiments that the Transcendental Meditation techniques are effective and have deep impacts on the personality of the practicing person. In this chapter, we have discussed what Transcendental Meditation is. In the next chapter we will discuss Transcendental and Regular Meditation.

Chapter 3: Transcendental vs. Regular Meditation

What Transcendental Meditation is not?

Although some basics are common is regular or normal meditation. But there are some main features that make Transcendental Meditation distinct and unique. Some people criticize that Transcendental Meditation is nothing but a regular meditation. But in reality, there is a difference between regular meditation and Transcendental Meditation. That In regular meditations we are required to concentrate on a concept or thing and it is a relaxing activity. On the other hand

Transcendental Meditation is different than a regular or normal meditation. Transcendental Meditation is a mantra based meditation and it is necessary to learn it through a trained and qualified teacher of Transcendental Meditation. The people who have practiced regular meditation and

Transcendental Meditation has found Transcendental Meditation very easy and relaxing experience. Practitioner of Transcendental Meditation highly recommends Transcendental Meditation as a way to get internal peace.

How Transcendental Meditation is different?

Following are some distinct features of Transcendental Meditation,

1.   The Transcendental Meditation technique as mentioned at TM.org is easy and works everyone.

2.   If we learn Transcendental Meditation from a certified and experienced Transcendental Meditation trainer then Transcendental Meditation always deliver results.

3.　　If you want them, time of free follow classes available for you

4.　　As many as 364 independently published peer-reviewed research studies that shed light on the importance of Transcendental Meditation. These studies futher go on to say that Transcendental Meditation technique positively affect the all aspect of a person's life.

5.　　Transcendental Meditation technique's certified trainers are widely available in almost all parts of the world, especially in the US and India. One great aspect of this Transcendental Meditation technique learning training is that the Transcendental Meditation technique teachers are always committed to teach you whether you pay as much they charge or not.

6.　　In different countries in general and the US particular there are help lines available that provide help on the phone. While in the US if you call 888-LearnTM, the Transcendental Meditation representative will locate a Transcendental Meditation technique trainer near you.

7.   There are a lot of resources on the internet to know about Transcendental Meditation techniques. But it is strongly recommended that you attend certified Transcendental Meditation technique trainers to master it.

In this chapter, we have discussed Transcendental and Regular Meditation. in the next chapter we will discuss What Happens During Transcendental Meditation.

Chapter 4: What Happens During Transcendental Meditation?

What Happens During Transcendental Meditation? is the most famous question of the general public. In fact Transcendental Meditation, as the work transcendental suggests, means during Transcendental Meditation busy surface thinking is transcended. Here the specific technique being used is so much important as the Transcendental Meditation technique creates the initial conditions for transcending to occur effortlessly. This is a natural phenomenon. Latest research studies on the Transcendental Meditation subject has focused on transcendental consciousness has shown that whole brain coherence occurs during Transcendental Meditation.

There are plenty of benefits of Transcendental Meditation and these benefits vary from highly ordered tendency of body and mind to highly ordered function in the coherence. Many people have found the Transcendental Meditation experience only fleetingly. By fleetingly we mean Transcendental Meditation experience's those pleasurable moments that sometime occur at the meeting point between normal meditation time and sleep.

Transcending occurs repeatedly in Transcendental Meditation depending upon the concentration and deeply involvement of the practitioners. Here, it is important to differentiate other meditation techniques and Transcendental Meditation technique. In regular meditation techniques, the practice solely relies on individual efforts. Most of the time, the regular meditations are just mental exercises that keep the mind attentive and active. Regular meditation exercises generally do not access the mind's natural inclination to surpass its own commotion. Oxygen consumption in body is a prime indicator of levels of rest and activity. So during Transcendental Meditation oxygen consumption becomes half and that decrease in oxygen occurs during night sleep. This is an amazing phenomenon that cannot be replicated in other exercises. On contrary normal exercises increase the oxygen consumption in the body. Effort or concentration cannot render deeply refreshing state like this. It is the nature alone that can do this for you. It would not be wrong if you think that, why does the body need less oxygen during Transcendental Meditation? The answer to this question is simple. As we have discussed earlier in this book that Transcendental Meditation is energizing and mindful experience if practice as per the training from a certified instructor.

During Transcendental Meditation exercise, the body adopts a more energy-efficient style of functioning. Moreover, during this exercise, the arteries get bigger so that more blood flows with less effort. While heart beat rate decreases, the volume of lactic acid, the biochemical associated with anxiety, drops markedly. Further anxiety state is decreased by electrical skin resistance and electrical skin resistance rises sharply.

Again, individual effort cannot render this integrated complex of changes in mind and body of human being, it is naturally powered phenomenon. That is why the body automatically neutralizes accumulated stress in this state of least excitation. It further helps remove physical abnormalities and carries out repairs and renewals. In other words, "It is the opposite of the primitive, now obsolete, fight-or-flight response, which can lead to hypertension if frequently provoked by the fast pace of modern life. "

Some people say that they would not be ale to sit still for a long time for Transcendental Meditation. Naturally, the tendency of mind is to transcend. It is due to the fact the settling down of both mind and body occur automatically. In essence, apart from other mental and physical benefits, Transcendental Meditation experience is enjoyable and pleasurable. This is the most important aspect of Transcendental Meditation that attracts the general people towards Transcendental Meditation. In this chapter, we have discussed what happens during Transcendental Meditation. In the next chapter we will discuss how do we know Transcendental Meditation is working?

Chapter 5: How do we know Transcendental Meditation is working?

Whether Transcendental Meditation is working with you or not is so much easy. Transcendental Meditation techniques are very much affective and the person who is practicing Transcendental Meditation in a right manner can observe the affects of Transcendental Meditation soon after starting it. Some people start observing the results of Transcendental Meditation after some time. Some people do not observe affects of Transcendental Meditation after a long time. If a person is not observing the affects of Transcendental Meditation over a period of time then he or she must consult his or her trainer because may be he or she is not following the right methods.

Research and science

The mental and body needs of every person are different than that of others but most of the practitioners benefiting through Transcendental Meditation. Research and Science have also proved that Transcendental Meditation is an effective method to keep oneself calm and patient. We will discuss the effects of Transcendental Meditation proved by science in detail in the next chapter. The next chapter will discuss the effects of Transcendental Meditation on human being in general and the brain on human beings in particular in the light of science and many research studies.

People have found a lot of benefits through practicing Transcendental Meditation techniques. People with anxiety, depression and stress problems have found a cure through Transcendental Meditation. Moreover, the people with a range of mental and physical disabilities have also found amazing things in Transcendental Meditation. In this chapter, we have discussed how we know that Transcendental Meditation is working. In the next chapter we will discuss Transcendental Meditation effect on the brain.

Many researchers have revealed that Transcendental Meditation is mindful. The mindfulness is very important ability to be aware of your body, mind and feelings. Mindfulness help your each and every routine work. It is important to note that some people overly exaggerate the benefits and effects of Transcendental Meditation to promote it. It is possible that they really have achieved some amazing results that generally are not achievable. Also the chances are that person is exaggerating the benefits and importance of Transcendental Meditation.

Chapter 6: Transcendental Meditation Effects on the Brain

There are a lot of research studies that have studied the role of Transcendental Meditation techniques on the brain. Mind and Brain, the Journal of Psychiatry has published research studies that elaborate the impact of Transcendental Meditation on the brain of human beings. A random-assignment controlled study published in 2013 in Mind & Brain, The Journal of Psychiatry (Vol 2, No 1) found "improved brain functioning and decreased symptoms of attention-deficit/hyperactivity disorder, ADHD, in students practicing the Transcendental Meditation technique. The paper, ADHD, Brain functioning, and Transcendental Meditation Practice, is the most recent study demonstrating TM's ability to help students with attention-related difficulties." Following are the excerpts from the discussions with experts regarding Transcendental Meditation Practice.

A study that was conducted, on children of language based learning disability, over a period of 6 months in an independent school in Washington, DC. The students practicing in the Transcendental Meditation technique showed improved brain functioning. They also showed increased brain processing and improved language-based skills among ADHD. Electroencephalogram (EEG) tests performed to measure the electrical activity of students' brains as they performed a demanding computer-based visual-motor task by Neuroscientist Fred Travis, Ph.D., and other researchers. Successful performance of the task required attention, focus, memory, and impulse control.

ADHD students practicing the meditation technique improved brain performance, processing and improved language based skills, the study showed. Moreover, students were tested for a verbal fluency test. The purpose of this test was to measure higher order executive functions that include initiation, simultaneous processing, and systematic retrieval of knowledge. Several fundamental cognitive components were the basis of Performance of this task. These fundamental cognitive components include vocabulary knowledge, spelling, and attention. Experts say that EEG measurement can help to diagnose ADHD as the ratio of theta brain waves can be used to accurately identify students with ADHD from those without it.

"In normal individuals, theta activity in the brain during tasks suggests that the brain is blocking out irrelevant information so the person can focus on the task," said Travis. "But in individuals with ADHD, the theta activity is even higher, suggesting that the brain is also blocking out relevant information." And when beta activity, which is associated with focus, is lower than normal, Travis added, "It affects the ability to concentrate on task for extended periods of time."

"Prior research shows ADHD children have slower brain development and a reduced ability to cope with stress," said co-researcher William Stixrud, Ph.D., a prominent

Silver Spring, Maryland, clinical neuropsychologist. "Virtually everyone finds it difficult to pay attention, organize themselves and get things done when they're under stress," he said. "Stress interferes with the ability to learn—it shuts down the brain. Functions such as attention, memory, organization, and integration are compromised."

Why the TM Technique?

"We chose the TM technique for this study because studies show that it increases brain function and reduces stress. We wanted to know if it would have a similar effect in the case of ADHD, and if it did, would that also improve the symptoms of ADHD," said principal investigator Sarina J. Grosswald, Ed.D., a George Washington University-trained cognitive learning specialist. Dr. Stixrud added, "Because stress significantly compromises attention and all of the key executive functions such as inhibition, working memory, organization, and mental flexibility, it made sense that a technique that can reduce a child's level of stress should also improve his or her cognitive functioning."

Transcendental Meditation technique is an easy and simple practice. It is unique among categories of meditation. "TM does not require concentration, controlling the mind or disciplined focus—challenges for anyone with ADHD," said Dr. Grosswald. "What's significant about these new findings," Grosswald said, "is that among children who have difficulty with focus and attention, we see the same results. The fact that these children are able to do TM, and do it easily, shows us that this technique may be particularly well-suited for children with ADHD."

Previous researches have revealed that, "during Transcendental Meditation there is a unique experience of 'restful alertness' in mind and body, an experience associated with higher metabolic activity in the frontal and parietal parts of the brain, indicating alertness, along with decreased metabolic activity in the thalamus, which is involved in regulating arousal, and hyperactivity. This restfully alert brain state becomes more present outside of meditation as a result of daily Transcendental Meditation practice, allowing ADHD students to attend to tasks."

"While stimulant medication is very beneficial for some of my clients with ADHD," adds Dr. Stixrud, "the number of children who receive great benefit from medicine with minimal side-effects is relatively small. The fact that TM appears to improve attention and executive functions, and significantly reduces stress with no negative side-effects, is clearly very promising." In this chapter, we have discussed Transcendental Meditation effect on the brain. In the next chapter we will discuss Techniques for Transcendental Meditation.

Chapter 7: Techniques for Transcendental Meditation

The following frequently asked question are taken from Transcendental Meditation techniques teaching website,

What can TM do for me?

Well, it can do amazing things with you and it can make your life much more pleasurable and balanced. People who have developed the skill to practice Transcendental Meditation, assert that this technique has a transforming effect. These people report a lot of objectives they have achieved which include but not limited to reducing stress and anxiety, mood disorders, insomnia, and hypertension, etc. Persistent stress is damaging to health, happiness, creativity, and productivity. More than 350 published research studies on effectiveness of Transcendental Meditation technique for stress and stress-related conditions, brain function proved these facts.

What is the TM technique?

Regardless of the plenty of benefits of Transcendental Meditation it is true that it is a simple and natural technique. It can be practiced as low as 20 minutes two times each day while sitting still with the eyes closed. Transcendental Meditation is a next generation mediation that helps practitioners find answer to questions raised by their problems coupled with an enjoyable and refreshing experience. Transcendental Meditation is neither a religious or philosophical concept, nor it is a lifestyle. More than six million people have learned it which include people of all ages, cultures, and religions around the world.

What if I'm not good at controlling my mind?

It is alright is you are not able to concentrate in the start. In fact, Transcendental Meditation does not require no concentration, no control of the mind, no reflection, no monitoring of thoughts. Anyone can do it well. Even with disabilities like ADHD and TSD has done it well. It is because of the reason that the Transcendental Meditation technique easily allows the active mind to become normal to a state of inner peace and calm.

What happens when you meditate?

The Transcendental Method technique helps your mind to settle inward. It happens through quieter levels of thought. It continues until you experience pure consciousness, which is the most silent and peaceful level of your own attentiveness and consciousness. And this is known as automatic self-transcending.

What if I'm skeptical?

It is natural that we often not believe without observing a thing. It is not necessary prerequisite of Transcendental Meditation to have full faith in its effectiveness. You can start it and you will experience its effectiveness by the passage of time.

Can I learn TM from a book, DVD, or online?

It is true that Transcendental Meditation is easy to practice but it does not mean that it is easy to learn from scratch too. Imagine learning to play a guitar or learning to play golf and how easy it would be to learn from a experienced teacher than that of learning yourself. May be you have got amazing learning skills but the point here is a experienced teacher can make you learn Transcendental Meditation in less time than that of a self learning stint. The Transcendental Meditation technique is easy to learn but demands personalized interactive supervision. That is why it can be better learned through one-on-one instruction by a certified Transcendental Meditation teacher. On the other hand, various books, websites, DVDs, etc. are available in the market, no doubt these materials can help you a lot but none of them teaches a certified Transcendental Meditation teacher.

What is TM's value in daily life?

Extensive peer-reviewed published research on the TM technique has found a wide range of wellness benefits including:

- It gives greater inner peace the whole day

- It decreases Cortisol (stress hormone)

- It normalize blood pressure

- It reduces insomnia

- It decreases risk of heart attack and stroke

- It decreases anxiety, stress and depression

- It makes brain and memory functions better

You can contact your local certified Transcendental Meditation teacher to learn more about Transcendental Meditation techniques. Moreover, there are plenty of websites that are offering free resources on Transcendental Meditation topic. Following lines are taken from an important study on Transcendental Meditation,

"According to a report published in the Journal of Alternative and Complementary Medicine, a meta-analysis of TM analyzed 16 trials and 1,295 participants. The conclusion was that TM worked better in reducing severe anxiety than psychotherapy or other relaxation techniques... As a bonus, TM also produced lower blood pressure, better sleep, improved family life, less substance abuse and a better employment situation."

Transcendental Meditation Teacher Training

Transcendental Meditation is growing rapidly nowadays. Although is not difficult to practice but, nevertheless, people are sparing time to learn it. Some people are relying on books and internet to learn it. Many people are watching video tutorials to effectively practice the Transcendental Meditation. On the other hand, a lot of people around the world are getting its training from different trainers and institutes to get best out of Transcendental Meditation. Transcendental Meditation's official website offers some resources to learn this amazing thing. There are a large number of books on this subject and counting. Moreover, there are countless websites that are offering free resources for everyone. In this chapter, we have discussed the techniques for transcendental meditation. In the next chapter we will discuss why Transcendental Meditation works for everyone.

Chapter 8: Why Transcendental Meditation Works for Everyone?

It is reality that Transcendental Meditation method works for everyone. There are plenty of reasons behind this fact. One of the reason behind this fact is Transcendental Medication is so simple, natural and effortless to practice. That is why even children from the as low as 6 years old can learn it. You are never too old to learn Transcendental Meditation! Anyone who can think can practice Transcendental Meditation!

Transcendental Meditation stimulates natural processes in human mind and body. And it is a well established fact that all human beings have same body and mind structure. For some people it will render results straight away and sometimes in a spectacular way. On the other hand, some people will have to wait to wait a bit longer. May be it is because of the fact that due to age, culture and social differences people come up with variety of problems and the time to solve that problem varies accordingly. Sooner or later it starts working if practiced in a right way. If a person is practicing it since long, then he must consult his teacher may be his method of practicing Transcendental Meditation is not as right as it should be.

Another reason people are adopting Transcendental Meditation is the fact that they do not have to give up anything to start Transcendental Meditation. May be your teacher ask you to give up anything to easily learn Transcendental Meditation but that is a different issue. It is true that some things have to leave to control your mind easily. It is important to note that good habits are desirable to learn Transcendental Meditation but good habits are not a prerequisite to learn Transcendental Meditation. A major question about having sex comes to minds of the people who are thinking to start Transcendental Meditation. But people can start practicing Transcendental Meditation without leaving it. People from any addiction and obsession can start Transcendental Meditation but by the passage of time they may experience decrease in some bad habit. It is because the Transcendental Meditation is itself an alternative method of enjoyment and relaxation.

Some people think that the purpose of Transcendental Meditation is just to still and calm the body and mind for some time. Before learning Transcendental Meditation it is general thinking of the people but the reality is different. By the passage of time people get to know real motive behind Transcendental Meditation. Moreover, no effort is needed to concentrate or control the mind because it is the nature of the mind to be active. Our mind also stays still if we want to keep it still. It is just the matter of time and you will learn how to mediate soon after practicing Transcendental Meditation. Even people with mental and physical disabilities have practiced Transcendental meditation successfully.

You only have to spare maximum 20 minutes for Transcendental Meditation. Do Transcendental Meditation twice a day. It is the maximum time recommended to give you the benefits you would get from hours of most other techniques. If you cannot spare 40 minutes a day you will still get enormous benefit by sparing as much time as you easily can. Transcendental Meditation is very pleasurable, mindful and enjoyable and easy to do. You will later be able to spare more and more time for it right after starting experiencing its benefits. You will find keeping it up much easier than anything else you've tried. Another important aspect is that you can practice Transcendental Meditation anywhere and anytime. The people who start benefitting from Transcendental Meditation have said that they spared just 40 minutes per day and gained hours against that 40 minutes. It is because when we come out of meditation become more and more attentive to all the matters and stays calm and focused.

Because of the reason that the process Transcendental Meditation stimulates is natural it will always work for everyone. Some people start observing its benefits immediately whereas, others take some time to see its benefits. If it takes too long and not show results then it is necessary that your consult with your trainer. May be you are missing some important aspect to be considered. It will work for all because people from different religion have learned Transcendental Meditation successfully.

Moreover these people from all religions are getting benefits by practicing Transcendental Meditation. The teachers of Transcendental Meditation are Christian, Jewish, Muslim, Hindu, Buddhist etc. Priests, Monks, Nuns and even a few Bishops have learned transcendental meditation. The most common comment is that it has enriched their faith. Transcendental Meditation is not a religious belief or religion but Yoga which is spiritual knowledge or personal and subjective. There is a distinct difference, and Yoga pre-dates religion by thousands of years. For completely understanding this concept or if you have someone near you who thinks Transcendental Meditation is a threat to their beliefs then refer to a wonderful book written by a Catholic Priest, the late Fr. Adrian Smith, which gives a Christian understanding of Transcendental Meditation. It iss called 'A Key to the Kingdom of Heaven'. He has also authored a pamphlet entitled "Questions Christians ask about transcendental meditation". So these and other books are also available to satisfy your curiosity.

It is a natural process that is why it is safe and cannot harm anyone. It gives deep rest to both mind and body. This rest will gradually decrease mental problems and give greater mental stability. Transcendental Meditation will help you get full benefits of this technique. People with disabilities can also practice Transcendental Meditation but they need to do some additional things which their instructor would tell them. We may make some adjustments to the teaching to take mental illness into account, so you are requested to make this clear to your teacher on the teacher's information form before instruction. It is a distinguishing feature of Transcendental Meditation that the trainers and teachers give full and one-to-one attention to all students.

In this chapter, we have discussed why transcendental meditation works for all. In the next part of the book, we will summarize the whole discussion of this book.

Famous Practitioners of Transcendental Meditation

Over a couple of last decades the fan following of Transcendental Meditation is growing at rapidly. A large number of famous personalities and celebrities are practitioners of Transcendental Meditation. The practitioners of Transcendental Meditation belong to different parts of the world. The Transcendental Meditation community is very diverse in terms of faith, educational qualification, profession, geographical location and cultures background. It is most popular in Western cultures and Hindu cultures and Buddhist cultures. Even the Transcendental Meditation is equally famous among the people who do not believe in GOD or any religion. Although the complete list of famous people is very long, but following is a list of notable and most famous personalities and celebrities,

- Tosin Abasi, guitarist

- Paula Abdul, singer, dancer, choreographer

- Johari Abdul-Malik, Muslim chaplain

- Omar Akram, Afghan-American recording artist

- Rupert Allason, military historian, politician, writer

- Jennifer Aniston, actress

- Judd Apatow, film producer

- India Arie, singer-songwriter

- Arthur Ashe, professional tennis player

- Jane Asher, actress, author, entrepreneur

- Jennifer Ashton, physician, author

- Ramani Ayer, business executive

B

- Angelo Badalamenti, soundtrack composer

- Yeojin Bae, fashion designer

- Michael Balzary (Flea), musician, Red Hot Chili Peppers

- Carole Bamford, businesswoman

- Sara Banerji, author

- Selby Baqwa, South Africa's first Public Protector

- Lionel Bart, composer

- Mario Batali, restaurateur

- Beth Behrs, actress

- Chrysta Bell, singer, model

- Kristen Bell, actress

- John G. Bennett, research director, author

- Itzhak Bentov, inventor, mystic and author

- Marisa Berenson, model, actress

- Robyn Berkley, fashion publicist, fashion designer

- Roger Berkowitz, restaurateur

- Gabrielle Bernstein, motivational speaker, author

- Richard Beymer, actor

- Buddy Biancalana, Major League Baseball

- Taddy Blecher, educational entrepreneur

- Harold H. Bloomfield, author

- Michael Booth, food and travel writer, journalist

- Larry Bowa, Major League Baseball

- Jenny Boyd, fashion model, sister of Pattie Boyd

- Pattie Boyd, fashion model, former wife of George Harrison and Eric Clapton

- Russell Brand, comedian, actor, author

- Jeff Bridges, actor, musician

- Steve Brill, naturalist, author

- Pete Broberg, Major League Baseball

- Jerry Brown, Governor of California

- Courtney Brown, social scientist

- Charles Bukowski, poet, novelist

- Gisele Bündchen, mode

- Mark Bunn, Australian rules footballer, author

- Tim Burgess, musician (The Charlatans)

C

- Tony Cárdenas, U.S. Congressman

- Flávio Canto, Olympic bronze medalist, judo

- Steve Carlton, Major League Baseball

- Wes Carr, Australian singer-songwriter

- Jim Carrey, actor, comedian, film producer

- Danielle Caruana, singer-songwriter

- Judy Chalfen, co-founder of Action for Children's Television

- Joaquim Chissano, former President of Mozambique

- Deepak Chopra, holistic health author

- Maureen Cleave, journalist

- Nick Clegg, Deputy Prime Minister of the United Kingdom

- Sarah Coakley, theologian

- Lynn Collins, actress[

- Stephen Collins, actor, writer, singer

- Nancy Cooke de Herrera, socialite, fashion expert, author

- Ellen Corby, actress

- Rita Cosby, television journalist

- Catherine E. Coulson, actress

- Anthony Cox, film producer

- Sheryl Crow, singer-songwriter

- Candy Crowley, journalist

D

- Rebecca Da Costa, actress

- Ray Dalio, hedge fund manager

- Hunter Davies, author, journalist

- Franklin M. Davis, Jr., major general, author

- Walter Day, Twin Galaxies founder

- Barbara De Angelis*, relationship consultant, author

- Ashley Deans*, physicist, educator

- Ellen DeGeneres, comedienne, television host

- Jimmy Demers, singer-songwriter

- Daniel Dennett, philosopher, cognitive scientist

- Kat Dennings, actress

- John Densmore, musician (The Doors)

- John Denver, singer-songwriter

- Laura Dern, actress, film director, producer

- Paul Dimattina, Australian Football League

- Meital Dohan, Israeli actress[

- Pete Dominick, comedian, talk radio personality

- Donovan, singer-songwriter, musician

- Bill Duke, actor, film director

- Doris Duke, tobacco heiress

- Lena Dunham, writer, director, actor

E

- Clint Eastwood, actor, film director

- Roy Eaton, pianist, advertising creative

- Mal Evans, road manager (The Beatles)

F

- Marianne Faithfull, singer, actress[

- Mia Farrow, actress

- Prudence Farrow*, film producer

- Marilyn Ferguson, writer

- Sky Ferreira, singer-songwriter, model, actress

- Noel Fielding, comedian

- Jane Fonda, actress, political activist, entrepreneur

- Nicola Formichetti, fashion director

- Ben Foster, actor

- Squire Fridell, actor

- Richard A. Friedman, psychiatrist

- Sadie Frost, actress

- Buckminster Fuller, engineer, author, inventor

- Deborra-Lee Furness, actress

G

- Greta Garbo, actress

- Jeff Garlin, comedian, actor, director

- Mac Gayden, musician, songwriter

- Adam Gaynor, musician

- Aileen Getty, heiress, activist

- Billy Gibbons, musician (ZZ Top)

- William Gibson, playwright and writer

- Rick Goings, chairman and CEO of Tupperware

- Jeff Goldblum, actor

- Nat Goldhaber*, venture capitalist, entrepreneur

- Heather Graham, actress

- John Gray*, author

- Judy Greer, actress, author

- Arlen F. Gregorio, politician

- Merv Griffin, singer, TV host

- Bruno Grollo, construction magnate

- Bill Gross, bond investor

- Jerry Grote, Major League Baseball

H

- John Hagelin*, particle physicist, Natural Law Party presidential candidate

- William Hague, First Secretary of State, former Foreign Secretary[

- George Hamilton, actor

- Ben Harper, singer-songwriter, musician

- George Harrison, musician (The Beatles)

- Olivia Harrison, author, film producer, wife of George Harrison

- John Harvey-Jones, business executive

- Goldie Hawn, actress

- Louise Hay, self-help author

- J. C. Hayward, news anchor

- Kevin Hearn, musician

- Doug Henning, magician

- Jim Henson, puppeteer

- Bill Hicks, comedian, musician[

- Steve Higgins, comedy writer

- Michael Hill, jeweler]

- Claire Hoffman, journalist

- Josh Homme, musician

- Jon Hopkins, musician, record producer

- Paul Horn*, musician

- Billy Howerdel, guitarist, songwriter]

I

- Elaine Ingham, soil microbiologist

- Sharon Isbin, musician

- V. R. Krishna Iyer, judge, minister of law

J

- Hugh Jackman, actor

- Mick Jagger, musician (The Rolling Stones)

- Jim James, lead vocalist (My Morning Jacket)

- Al Jardine, musician (The Beach Boys)

- Alfred L. Jenkins, diplomat, author

- Brian Josephson, physicist, Nobel laureate

K

- Mitch Kapor*, software and Internet entrepreneur

- Andy Kaufman*, actor, comedian

- Ryan Kavanaugh, film producer

- Miranda Kerr, mode

- Nicole Kidman, actress, singer, film producer

- Kevin Kimberlin, chairman Spencer Trask

- Zell Kravinsky*, investor

- Lenny Kravitz, singer-songwriter, record producer

- Robby Krieger, musician (The Doors)

- Igor Kufayev, artist, spiritual teacher

L

- John La Fave, politician

- Royston Langdon, musician

- Bettye LaVette, singer-songwriter

- Lois Lee, founder and president Children of the Night

- Peggy Lee, singer, actress, composer

- Júlia Lemmertz, actress

- Cynthia Lennon, wife of John Lennon]

- John Lennon, musician (The Beatles)

- Sean Lennon, musician

- David Letterman, comedian and talk show host

- Ramsey Lewis, composer, musician]

- Henry Lewy, sound engineer, record producer

- Lykke Li, singer-songwriter

- Eli Lieb, singer-songwriter

- Charles Lloyd, musician

- Dan Loeb, hedge fund manager

- Jim Lonborg, Major League Baseball player]

- Nancy Lonsdorf, author, physician

- Mike Love*, singer-songwriter, musician (The Beach Boys)

- Daisy Lowe, model and actress

- George Lucas, film producer

- Steve Lukather, musician (Toto)

- David Lynch, film director, artist

- Jennifer Lynch, screenwriter, director

M

- Shirley MacLaine, actress, dancer

- Leon MacLaren, barrister, politician, philosopher

- Shrikar Madiraju, film director

- Madonna, singer-songwriter, actress

- Martie Maguire, musician (Dixie Chicks)

- Natalie Maines, singer-songwriter (Dixie Chicks)

- Kellee Maize, rapper, songwriter

- Ray Manzarek, musician (The Doors)

- Pete Maravich, NBA player

- Henry Marsh, pop musician, composer

- Claudia Mason, model, actress

- Brent Mayne, Major League Baseball

- James McCartney, musician

- Paul McCartney, musician (The Beatles)

- Willie McCovey, Major League Baseball

- Rose McGowan, actress

- Marshall McLuhan, educator, philosopher

- Peter McWilliams, writer

- Eva Mendes, actress, model

- Miguel, recording artist

- Alyssa Miller, model

- Tom Miller, performance artist

- Gyp "Gypsy Dave" Mills, sculptor, songwriter

- Moby, musician

- Melba Moore, singer, actress

- Mary Tyler Moore, actress

- Wagner Moura, actor

- Tainá Müller, actress, model

- Rupert Murdoch, media mogul

N

- Tony Nader*, neuroscientist, researcher, TM movement leader

- Joe Namath, professional football player

- Martina Navratilova, tennis professional

- Richard Nolan, politician

- B. J. Novak, actor, comedian

O

- Soledad O'Brien, American broadcast journalist

- Rosie O'Donnell, actress, comedienne, author

- Mike Oldfield, musician, composer

- David Orme-Johnson*, professor, TM researcher

- Mehmet Oz, surgeon, TV host, writer

P

- Tim Page, music critic

- Gwyneth Paltrow, actress

- Ron Parker*, politician (Natural Law Party)

- Jeff Peckman*, politician, UFOlogist

- Katy Perry, singer-songwriter, actress

- Tom Petty, musician

- Gary Player, professional golfer

- Priscilla Presley, actress

R

- Josh Radnor, actor, film director, screenwriter

- Rene Rancourt, singer

- Nancy Redd, HuffPost Live host

- Greg Reitman, documentary filmmaker

- Burt Reynolds, actor

- Bill Robinson, Major League Baseball

- Smokey Robinson, singer-songwriter

- Nouriel Roubini, economist

- Dilma Rousseff, President of Brazil

- Norman Rosenthal, psychiatrist, research scientist, author

- Jonathan Rowson, chess grandmaster

- Rick Rubin, record producer

- Peter Russell, physicist, author

S

- Sheri Salata, co-president OWN, president Harpo Productions

- Santigold (Santi White), musician

- Rodrigo Santoro, actor

- Juan Manuel Santos, President of Colombia

- Susan Sarandon, actress

- Vidal Sassoon, hairdresser, businessman

- Tony Schwartz, writer

- Arnold Schwarzenegger, bodybuilder, actor, businessman, politician

- Martin Scorsese, film director

- William Scranton III*, Lieutenant Governor of Pennsylvania

- Jerry Seinfeld, comedian, actor, writer

- Lesley Jane Seymour, editor-in-chief More

- Sri Sri Ravi Shankar, spiritual leader

- Rupert Sheldrake, scientist, author

- Dax Shepard, actor, comedian

- Swami Shyam, (Shyam Shrivastava) spiritual leader

- Kimora Lee Simmons, model, entrepreneur

- Russell Simmons, entrepreneur

- Matt Skiba, musician (Alkaline Trio)

- Chas Smash, musician (Madness)

- Jeffrey M. Smith, activist

- Andrew Ross Sorkin, journalist, author

- Willie Stargell, Major League Baseball

- Maureen Starkey, first wife of Ringo Starr

- Ringo Starr, musician (The Beatles)

- Suzanne Steinbaum, cardiologist

- George Stephanopoulos, television journalist, political advisor

- Ali Stephens, model

- Howard Stern, radio personality, actor, author

- Beth Ostrosky Stern, TV personality, actress, model

- Natalie Stewart, singer-songwriter

- Sting, musician

- Trudie Styler, producer, actress, wife of Sting

- Andrew Sullivan, author, editor, political commentator

- Patrick Swayze, actor

T

- Sam Taylor-Wood, filmmaker, photographer, visual artist

- Christos Tolera, musician, artist

- Mike Tompkins*, polititican (Natural Law Party)

- Liv Tyler, actress

U

- Del Unser, Major League Baseball player

V

- Steve Vai, guitarist, composer

- Eddie Vedder, musician (Pearl Jam)

- Kurt Vonnegut, author

W

- Alice Walker, novelist, poet, Pulitzer Prize winner

- Bill Walton, professional basketball, sportscaster

- David Ware, jazz musician

- Naomi Watts, actress

- Dee Dee Wilde, dancer (Pan's People)

- Marianne Williamson, author, lecturer, philanthropist

- Brian Wilson, musician (The Beach Boys)

- Dennis Wilson, musician (The Beach Boys)

- Oprah Winfrey, American media proprietor, talk show host

- James Wolcott, journalist

- Stevie Wonder, singer-songwriter, producer, musician, activist

- C. V. Wood, chief developer of Disneyland

- Jim Wright, US congressman and Speaker of the House

- Syreeta Wright*, singer-songwriter

Z

- Efrem Zimbalist, Jr., actor

- Raquel Zimmermann, mode

- Barry Zito, Major League Baseball

- ˈItalo Zucchelli, Italian fashion designer

Famous Quotes about Transcendental Medication

"Dedicating some time to meditation is a meaningful expression of caring for yourself that can help you move through the mire of feeling unworthy of recovery. As your mind grows quieter and more spacious, you can begin to see self-defeating thought patterns for what they are, and open up to other, more positive options."

Sharon Salzberg

"If you're studying for an exam you're not thinking about the results. If you're always worried about the results, you can't study a lot. So to be engaged and detached from the outcome is excellent. Excellence is behavior. I mean, isn't that what martial arts is about? And that's what meditation is about, that's what, in many ways, sports are about."

Deepak Chopra

"If you truly get in touch with a piece of carrot, you get in touch with the soil, the rain, the sunshine. You get in touch with Mother Earth and eating in such a way, you feel in touch with true life, your roots, and that is meditation. If we chew every morsel of our food in that way we become grateful and when you are grateful, you are happy."

Thich Nhat Hanh

"Transcendental meditation is an ancient mental technique that allows any human being to dive within, transcend and experience the source of everything. It's such a blessing for the human being because that eternal field is a field of unbounded intelligence, creativity, happiness, love, energy and peace."

David Lynch

"Meditation is to dive all the way within, beyond thought, to the source of thought and pure consciousness. It enlarges the container, every time you transcend. When you come out, you come out refreshed, filled with energy and enthusiasm for life."

"Life is all business. Spend your energy to get joy, happiness, evolution, and to gain more ability to enjoy. In this field we spend our energy. We never use our time, energy, speech, or ability to do something that doesn't help us grow and improve our life. It's not worth it."

Maharishi Mahesh Yogi

"It is the purity of man's heart and mind, and his innocent and faithful approach to action with the purpose of all good to everyone, which really succeeds in yielding maximum results with minimum effort."

"Empty your mind, be formless, shapeless - like water. Now you put water into a cup, it becomes the cup, you put water into a bottle, it becomes the bottle, you put it in a teapot, it becomes the teapot. Now water can flow or it can crash. Be water, my friend."

"After sleeping through a hundred million centuries we have finally opened our eyes on a sumptuous planet, sparkling with color, bountiful with life. Within decades we must close our eyes again. Isn't it a noble, an enlightened way of spending our brief time in the sun, to work at understanding the universe and how we have come to wake up in it? This is how I answer when I am asked-as I am surprisingly often-why I bother to get up in the mornings."

"Meditation brings wisdom; lack of mediation leaves ignorance. Know well what leads you forward and what hold you back, and choose the path that leads to wisdom."

Conclusion

At the end of the book it is time to summarize all the discussion of the book. Majority of us know that the traditional act of meditation is present in Hinduism and Buddhism. Both Hinduism and Buddhism are of the view that very amazing results can be obtained by practicing meditation sincerely. It is not a mere claim. The process of meditation is indeed amazing experience that enriches the practitioner with spiritual energy.

Meditation also caters the need of human beings to obtain internal peace and peace of mind through a regular session of meditation on daily basis. Although meditation refers to a simple method of sitting with eyes closed for several minutes but nevertheless, there are different methods to practice mediation. These methods differ slightly from each other. So after a series of research on meditation, Mr. Maharishi Mahesh Yogi (1918-2008), from modern day India, introduced a new form of meditation known as Transcendental Meditation in the mid 1950s.

The Transcendental Meditation Movement spread at a very fast pace that it is practiced by millions of practitioners around the world. This book starts with a brief history of Transcendental Meditation and tells us that where it came from. Then is focuses on what is Transcendental Meditation. Then it sheds light on Transcendental Meditation vs. Regular Meditation issue.

Then it describes what Transcendental Meditation is not. Later it has explained how Transcendental Meditation is different and what happens during Transcendental Meditation. It also explains whether how we know Transcendental Meditation is working. Later we will discuss what research and science says about Transcendental Meditation followed by effects Transcendental Meditation on the brain. Techniques for Transcendental Meditation make this book unique and valuable. In the last part, this book discusses why Transcendental Meditation works for everyone. Famous Practitioners Transcendental Meditation and Famous

Quotes on Transcendental Meditation are also mentioned to motivate our readers.

Over a couple of last decades the fan following of Transcendental Meditation is growing at rapidly. A large number of famous personalities and celebrities are practitioners of Transcendental Meditation. The practitioners of Transcendental Meditation belong to different parts of the world. The Transcendental Meditation community is very diverse in terms of faith, educational qualification, profession, geographical location and cultures background. It is most popular in Western cultures and Hindu cultures and Buddhist cultures. Even the Transcendental Meditation is equally famous among the people who do not believe in GOD or any religion.

20202777R00046

Made in the USA
San Bernardino, CA
01 April 2015